MONEY WANTS ME!

Money Wants Me!

SHIRLEY A. SMOLKO

Henry H. Brown

Cavallaro Publishing

CONTENTS

Money Wants Me!

Printed in the U.S.A.

First Printing, 2022

Second Printing, 2023

ISBN: 978-1-958104-00-2

Library of Congress Control Number: 2022907829

Cavallaro Publishing
North Venice, Florida
www.cavallaropub.com
cavallaropub@gmail.com

DISCLAIMER

This book contains material from a distant time, which may not be gender neutral or sensitive. Therefore, all pronouns shall be deemed to refer to the masculine, feminine, neuter, singular or plural, wherever used herein, a pronoun in the masculine gender shall be considered as including the feminine gender.

The publisher and the author do not make any guarantees or other promises as to any results that may be obtained from using the contents of this book. To the maximum extent permitted by law, the publisher and the author disclaim any and all liability in the event any information, commentary, analysis, opinions, advice and/or recommendations contained in this book prove to be inaccurate, incomplete or unreliable, or result in any losses.

In summary, you understand that we make absolutely no guarantees as a result of applying this information, as well as the fact that you are solely responsible for the results of any action taken on your part as a result of any given information.

Part One By Shirley Smolko

~ 1 ~

INTRODUCTION

The Good Fairy

Once upon a time, a Good Fairy with a magic wand distributed rewards among mortals. To one man she gave jewels, another honor, and a third influence—to others renown, peace, and power, as each requested. Finally, she came to one who wanted nothing that any of the others had asked for.

> "Are you not pleased with the things others have chosen?" inquired the Good Fairy.

> "It's not things that I seek—it's the power to do things that I want," the man answered.

"Oh! You are a wise and far-seeing mortal who has avoided the ways of the foolish," exclaimed the fairy.

She lowered her wonder-working wand and told the mortal to open his hand, and money appeared. Suddenly, the gates of wealth swung wide open. Then she said, "The purpose of money in life is to help you open the doors to opportunity—the opportunity to enjoy the things money can buy; the opportunity for self-actualization; and the opportunity to help others. How will you use your money?"

~ 2 ~

THE FIRST CAUSE OF
MONEY

The first cause of money can be used by anyone regardless of religious or nonreligious beliefs. It is this first cause—the Original Force—that moves the planets, starts life on Earth, animates the body, builds houses, puts souls into people, and makes them think. The soul of man—the part of us that survives physical death—is an emanation of the Original Force of the Universe. If it were possible to stop this vitalizing force in the universe, everything, including man, would chill, wither, and die.

So then, it is the presence of the Original Force throughout the world that warms, invigorates, enlivens, and makes vital what would otherwise be cold, dead, and empty. It is this potent force that warms the soil in the springtime, sends sap up the trees, causes buds to bloom, perfumes flowers, and colors their beautiful petals. Everything that exists in life is an expression of the Original Force.

In his book, Creative Mind & Success, Earnest Holmes wrote the following passage about the expression of life and how it relates to money:

> *If all is an expression of life, then money is an expression of life and, as such, must be good. Without a certain amount of it in this life, we would have a hard time. But how to get it; that is the [human] race problem. How shall we acquire wealth? Money didn't make itself, and not being self-creative, it must be an effect. Behind it must be the cause that projects it. That cause is never seen; no cause is ever seen. Consciousness is the cause, and people who have a money consciousness have the outward expression of it. People who have it as a sure reality in their minds also have it as an expression in their pockets. People who don't have this mental likeness don't have money in their pockets.*

What we need to do is acquire a money consciousness. This may seem very material, but the true idea of money is not material—it is spiritual. We need to make our unity with it. We can never do this while we hold it away from us by thinking that we don't have it. Let us change the method and begin to make our unity with supply by daily declaring that all the power in the universe is daily bringing to us all that we can use. Feel the presence of supply. Know that it is yours now.

~ 3 ~

THE MIND

Psychologist discovered long ago that the total mind of man can be divided into two basic parts, the conscious and subconscious, as shown in the following diagram:

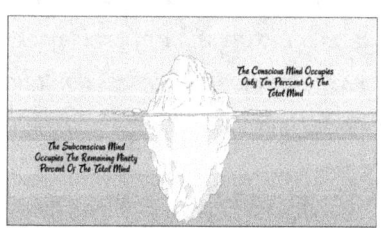

The Total Mind
Shirley Smolko

THE CONSCIOUS MIND

The conscious part of your mind—which comprises only ten percent of your total mind—is the part that tastes, hears, smells, feels, sees, talks, thinks, decides, laughs, cries, and plays. In other words, the conscious mind is the "active" part of the total mind, and it can direct and control the subconscious mind, which is "passive" and ready to receive direction from the conscious.

The conscious part of man's mind is the storehouse of his external knowledge, and the seat of that intelligence through which he exercises his sense of reasoning, analyzing, and will. Conscious intelligence is directly and indirectly influenced by some or all of the five physical senses. As long as these senses are active, the conscious mind cannot be restrained from reasoning since reasoning is its normal function. In contrast to the conscious mind, which is awake, the subconscious mind seems to be asleep, but it isn't. It never slumbers or sleeps.

THE SUBCONSCIOUS MIND

The subconscious mind automatically directs the functions of the body that go on without the direction or knowledge of the conscious mind. The Latin prefix *sub* means underneath; hence, the subconscious mind means the mind underneath the conscious mind. Your subconscious mind is responsible for the respiration of your lungs, the contraction of your heart, the rebuilding of the millions of tiny cells that make up your body, and the function of all your internal organs. It also directs your dreams, as well as other important aspects of your mentality. It is the seat of deeper constructive thought, memory, feelings, courage or fear, and instincts. It is also the nucleus of habitual happiness or chronic sorrow, hope or despair, good or bad motives, and the hidden resources for health, happiness, and success. The center of the higher spiritual faculties of the soul, such as intuition and moral sense, lies within the subconscious mind. It is the throne of God within us—the powerhouse of the universe—that is continuously manifesting our deepest beliefs. Instead of manifesting continuously by default, we can consciously tap this power to manifest our desires intentionally by reprogramming the subconscious mind with new beliefs.

When an impulse originates in the subconscious mind and rises to seek expression in the conscious mind, it crosses what has been called the *threshold of consciousness,* that imaginary line that separates consciousness from subconsciousness. You can just as easily direct ideas DOWN from your conscious mind into your subconscious mind as you can receive ideas UP from your subconscious mind.

The subconscious mind does not argue with the conscious mind. It accepts all thoughts, even if they are erroneous. The only way to overcome error thinking is to use strong counterthoughts, which the subconscious mind must accept. The thoughts we think over and over again become habits. It is no longer an act of judgment. The subconscious mind has creative power and will manifest the thoughts we give it. You can originate thoughts, and since thoughts are creative, you can create for yourself the things you desire.

THE CONSCIOUS MIND CAN CHOOSE

Whatever is observed through the senses of sight, smell, touch, taste, or hearing immediately conveys a definite impression to the conscious mind, which, having the power of will (and therefore the privilege of selection), can either accept or reject the impression. If the impression is accepted, it is instantly passed down to the subconscious mind for adoption. The subconscious mind then embraces the impression—whether good or evil—because the subconscious mind is not capable of analytical reasoning. It is controlled by the conscious mind. Therefore, you can readily see how important it is to maintain positive thoughts if you wish to exert a beneficial influence on your subconscious mind.

So the field of operations of the conscious mind is chiefly confined to what it perceives through the senses, and it is through the senses that it insists upon receiving proof. The conscious mind takes nothing for granted. But, once thoroughly satisfied, it conveys whatever may be its final convictions and conclusions to the subconscious mind, which, being unable to reason inductively, accepts them without the slightest resistance, whether they be correct and helpful or faulty and destructive.

Therefore, be very careful that you allow nothing harmful, depressing, discouraging, or unhealthy to reach your subconscious mind. Remember—it is impossible to convey any impression whatsoever to your subconscious mind without the impression first being accepted by your conscious mind. This is so, as already explained, because the conscious mind stands like a sentinel on guard at the entrance to your inner faculties and forbids the passing in of any idea unacceptable to it.

THE SUBCONSCIOUS IS AN OBEDIENT SERVANT

The subconscious mind freely accepts all suggestions furnished to it by the conscious mind. As clearly expounded by Mr. A. L. Allen in his *Message of New Thought*:

> *Through the law of suggestion, the subconscious, or subjective, mind submits to the thoughts and impressions it receives from the conscious, or objective, mind. These suggestions may be given either by yourself or by someone else. The subconscious mind registers the impression, which, over time, is given expression in the life and character of the individual. The subconscious mind will faithfully reproduce every mental idea or state contained in the impression. It is a rich soil, and the seed-thought planted in it by the conscious mind will produce according to its kind. If we plant flowers, we'll get flowers. If we sow tares, the crop will be tares. The subconscious is an obedient servant. It obeys the thoughts of the conscious mind. What it receives, it reproduces, and its effect is manifested in the personality of the individual. If we sow ideas of disease, we shall reap a harvest of disease. Thoughts of health will be re-expressed in healthy conditions. If we sow ideas of poverty, that will be our portion. If we sow thoughts of inferiority, weakness, and fear, we shall build a personality devoid of character and strength. Ideals of abundance will produce abundance if we enforce them with intelligence and energy.*

In his *Handbook of New Thought,* Mr. Horatio W. Dresser states it this way:

> *The conscious mind observes facts and applies them to general principles. The subconscious mind does not reason, but it receives and registers all impressions and affirmations suggested to it.*

The perceptions of reality received throughout one's life, through some or all of the physical senses, are the chief means for influencing the convictions of the subconscious mind. Each subsequent experience changes one's point of view to some degree. The things we see, the words we hear, the books we read, etc., are all parts of the material that help to determine the standpoint from which the subconscious mind reacts. Therefore, if the subconscious mind is trained through helpful ideas, good consequences will follow, but if it is permitted to absorb unhealthy ideas, injury will result in direct proportion to the individual's natural susceptibility.

A phrase often used in computer jargon, "Garbage In, Garbage Out," is a wonderful analogy of how we program our subconscious minds with unhealthy ideas and beliefs, often without even realizing it. If we program our minds with ideas and beliefs of lack and limitation, we will express poverty. On the other hand, if we program our minds with ideas and beliefs of abundance and opportunity, we will express wealth.

~ 4 ~

THE SUBCONSCIOUS PORTAL TO THE UNIVERSAL MIND

Prentice Mulford wrote about *The Supreme Power of the Universe* in many of his books; however, I think the following excerpt taken from his book, *The Gift of The Spirit,* provides the best synopsis:

A Supreme Power and Wisdom govern the Universe. The Supreme Mind is measureless and pervades endless space. Supreme Wisdom, Power, and Intelligence are in everything that exists from the atom to the planet.

The Supreme Power and Wisdom are more than in everything. The Supreme Mind is everything. The Supreme Mind is every atom of the mountain, the sea, the tree, the bird, the animal, the man, the woman. The Supreme Wisdom cannot be understood by man or by beings superior to man. But man will gladly receive the Supreme Thought and its wisdom, and let it work for happiness through him, caring not to fathom its mystery.

The Supreme Power has us in its charge, as it has the sun and endless systems of worlds in space. As we grow more to recognize this sublime and exhaustless wisdom, we will learn more and more to demand that wisdom, draw it to ourselves, make it a part of ourselves, and thereby be ever making ourselves newer and newer. This means ever-increasing wealth, greater and greater power to enjoy all that exists, gradual transition into a higher state of being, and the development of powers, which naturally belong to us.

Ralph Waldo Emerson wrote the following about our access to this power in the seventh chapter of his book *Nature:*

Who can set bounds to the possibilities of man? Once inhale the upper air, being admitted to behold the absolute natures of justice and truth, and we learn that man has access to the entire mind of the Creator, is himself the creator in the finite. This view, which admonishes me where the sources of wisdom and power lie, and points to virtue as to the golden key, which opens the palace of eternity,

There is one temple in the universe, and that is the body of man. We are the miracle of miracles, the great indescribable mystery of God. This miracle is wrapped up in the mystery of life, of which the conscious and subconscious workings of the mind are two of its most marvelous expressions. It is through the subconscious that we put ourselves in communion with the Universal Mind. It has been said that the Subconscious Mind is the great ocean of mental life, while the Conscious Mind is merely the ripple that washes against the shore. The fact that the subconscious mind is in communion with the great Universal Mind should fill us with a sense of confidence, power, and unlimited possibilities.

How can we tap into this unlimited World Force of the Universal Mind? As we have already seen, the subconscious mind is open to suggestions made by the conscious mind. Being immeasurably sensitive to impressions from without, the subconscious is incessantly receptive and subject to the influence of the conscious mind, when the latter is awake. In a figurative sense, the subconscious mind is the moving picture film or daily journal of the mind. It knows things, but it does not know how it knows them. It is the believing and faith mind, for it believes without requiring evidence. Being the embodiment of truth, it neither doubts nor asks questions, but takes for granted everything stated. It is the truthful, hopeful, trusting mind—the mind that predominates in the simple life of the child, for instance.

In his book, The Secret of the Ages, Robert Collier writes the following about the Universal Mind:

> *There is within you—within everyone—this mighty resistless force with which you can perform undertakings that will dazzle your reason, and stagger your imagination.*

There constantly resides within you a Mind that is all-wise, all-powerful, a Mind that is entirely apart from the mind that you consciously use in your everyday affairs yet which is one with it.

Your subconscious mind partakes of this wisdom and power, and it is through your subconscious mind that you can draw upon it in the attainment of anything you may desire. When you can intelligently reach your subconscious mind, you can be in communication with the Universal Mind.

Remember this: the Universal Mind is omnipotent. And since the subconscious mind is part of the Universal Mind, there is no limit to the things, which it can do when it is given the power to act. Given any desire that is in harmony with the Universal Mind and you have but to hold that desire in your thought to attract from the invisible domain the things you need to satisfy it.

The mind does its building solely by the power of thought. Its first requisite is a mental image, and your desire held with unswerving purpose will form that mental image. An understanding of this principle explains the power of prayer. The results of prayer are not brought about by some special dispensation of Providence. God is not a finite being to be cajoled or flattered into doing, as you desire. But when you pray earnestly you form a mental image of the thing that you desire and you hold it strongly in your conscious mind. Then the Universal Mind begins to work with and for you, and this is what brings about the manifestation that you desire.

The Universal Mind is all around you. It is as pervasive as the air you breathe. It encompasses you in the same way water encompasses fish in the sea. It seems hard to believe that a Mind busied with the immensities of the universe can consider such trivial affairs as our own when we are but one of the billions of forms of life that come into existence. Yet consider again the fish in the sea. It is no trouble for the sea to encompass them. It is no more trouble for the Universal Mind to encompass us. Its power, its thought, is as much at our disposal as the sunshine and the wind and the rain. Few of us fully take advantage of these great forces. Fewer still take advantage of the power of the Universal Mind. If you have any lack, if you are prey to poverty or disease, it is because you do not believe or do not understand the power that is yours.

~ 5 ~

YOU REAP THE MONEY
THOUGHTS YOU SOW

M any people are sincere in their desire to attain success in life but unwilling to contribute the mental elements necessary to realize success. Furthermore, they often prevent its realization by counterproductive beliefs and negative thoughts. All things are governed by an established energetic (spiritual) law. According to that law, every tree bears fruit after its kind, and every seed sown produces no other than its own kind. Likewise, if the condition of your conscious mind is positive and harmonious, it cannot help but produce good and beneficial results. On the contrary, if seeds of fear, doubt, and inferiority are sown, don't expect to reap a MONEY HARVEST! Within you exist all possibilities, so make the decision from this moment on that you will tap the unlimited riches of your subconscious mind.

BANISH FEARFUL THOUGHTS OF LACK & LIMITATION

Fear, the instinctive source of most evil, is often stimulated by a conscious mind that has been nurtured by false ideas and beliefs. Fear distorts the mind's reasoning, rendering it imperfect. When faced with obstacles and difficulties in life, don't look at such hindrances as unusual or unsurmountable; instead, consider their presence perfectly natural under the circumstances and determine how to best overcome them. Also, don't allow the conscious mind to become uneasy and magnify them. If you do, you are, through your own needless fear, helping to create failure.

Train your conscious mind to shield you from harmful influences. Its chief office is to reason intelligently and thus protect your subconscious mind by rejecting every injurious suggestion. It should also be trained to admit all helpful suggestions and permit your subconscious mind to receive them.

TURN AWAY FROM ADVERSE SUGGESTIONS

Not only is the subconscious mind susceptible to the influence of the conscious mind, but it is also susceptible to suggestions conveyed to it by others. Therefore, don't expose yourself to the negativity of others. Your conscious mind, which stands on guard at the entrance to your subconscious, must decide which suggestions may enter your subconscious. Only suggestions that are constructive and helpful—no matter how improbable they may seem—should be allowed to enter your subconscious mind.

Don't reason yourself out of the things to which you are entitled mentally, physically, and materially. "Can't" shouldn't be in your vocabulary. Affirm with all the positive force in you that you are a money magnet and that money wants you! An abundance of money to enjoy life is your birthright.

BELIEVE IN YOURSELF

People who constantly doubt themselves and others miss the greatest pleasures and benefits of life. So, develop faith in the inspirations of your subconscious mind, which is always in a creative mood. Train the conscious mind to give, but be sure that the suggestions it gives are constructive in nature and in keeping with your ideals of health, happiness, and success. If they are not, repudiate them as unworthy and destructive. In other words, do not limit your possibilities.

THINK POSITIVE MONEY THOUGHTS

Your thought is strong and potent beyond measure, but when you assume the 'wanting' attitude, although you do most certainly attract, it is nothing like the powerful attraction formed by your quiet, confident attitude of absolute conviction that the thing wants you. The attitude of desire is strong, but the attitude of certainty of possession —which this new thought makes possible—is a wonderful and veritable tower of strength. It has made possible to me things that had previously been impossible.

It is impossible to realize success with money if you continually expect failure. Do not entertain thoughts that are destructive or contrary to your desires. The thoughts you think are constantly being registered in your highly receptive subconscious mind—to haunt you later. Anxiety and doubt about your ability to attract money show that you have not accepted the fact that money wants you. Money cannot come to you until you have accepted this concept as a reality, so let go of any anxiety or apprehension that you may have regarding money. Rest in confidence, knowing that your subconscious mind is your own *genie in a bottle* and is able to manifest anything you desire.

~ 6 ~

THE HONEYPOT

I never weaken my position by affirming that I want anything. I say it wants me, and I know it will come. There is no use in making that statement, of course, if you doubt it. You must back up your statement with faith and feel it is already yours. It is rather on the principle of the honeypot and the swarm of summer bees: you are the pot of honey—dollars are the bees. The honey doesn't worry about the bees; it is content to be sweet and to give off a delicious scent. Bees make and eat honey! They need and want honey! They come from everywhere—even other hives—and swarm into it, sip its sweet nectar, and buzz all around. The honey has power—irresistible power so far as bees go—and they must have it! Say you run some particular line of business—you are the honey, and in the world, there are many people who want what you have to give them. They will gladly pay you money for it because they cannot help but be attracted to your honey.

The Honeypot Exercise

Step #1: Relaxing The Body & Mind Through Diaphragmatic Breathing

The first step in creative visualization is to relax your body and mind. Relaxing your body and mind allows you to achieve the Alpha brainwave level, which produces the perfect state for impressing your subconscious mind. Diaphragmatic breathing is the easiest way to achieve relaxation in preparation for your creative visualization session. You can perform this creative visualization either by sitting up or lying down.

To perform this exercise while sitting in a chair:

- Sit comfortably with your feet on the floor, and avoid slouching. Make sure your shoulders, head, and neck are relaxed.
- Place one hand on your upper chest and the other just below your rib cage. This will allow you to feel your diaphragm move as you breathe.
- Breathe in slowly through your nose so that your stomach moves out against your hand. The hand on your chest should remain as still as possible.
- Tighten your stomach muscles, letting them fall

inward as you exhale through pursed lips. The hand on your upper chest must remain as still as possible.

To perform this exercise while lying down:

- Lie on your back on a flat surface (or in bed) with your knees bent. You can use a pillow under your head and your knees for support if that's more comfortable.
- Place one hand on your upper chest and the other on your belly, just below your rib cage.
- Breathe in slowly through your nose, letting the air in deeply, towards your lower belly. The hand on your chest should remain still, while the one on your belly should rise.
- Tighten your abdominal muscles and let them fall inward as you exhale through pursed lips. The hand on your belly should move back to its original position.

Step #2: Honeypot Visualization

Imagine yourself as a honeypot, but instead of attracting bees, you attract money. Your thoughts of success and good fortune produce a sweet pheromone that Money cannot resist. See Money flowing to you from everywhere, especially through the money channels you have created. Say to yourself, Money wants me! Money wants me more than I want Money. Everything I do prospers, and avalanches of Money rain down upon me because Money wants me. Feel the intense love and attraction money has for you! With feeling and a conviction that it is so, make the following declaration to yourself often: Money Wants Me! Money Wants Me! Money Wants Me!

Part Two By Harry Brown

~ 7 ~

MONEY IS A MANIFESTATION OF THE ONE POWER

The Bane Of Poverty

P overty is caused by having a poverty consciousness. The only way to overcome poverty consciousness is to change negative beliefs regarding prosperity to positive ones. This change requires faith in yourself and the Universal Power, as well as a willingness to do the work required to make changes.

Most people believe that money is the source of all power, but it's not. This assumption must be replaced with the belief that ALL POWER IS IN ME, not money. Money is a human-made construct with power delegated to it by humans; therefore, it has no inherent power or value without humans. Although money has no inherent power, it represents supply. It stands in our thoughts for food, clothing, shelter, books, art, enjoyment, and the unfoldment of self-expression.

The Law of Opulence

Supplying human needs is the function of the universe. Everything is for everyone. The sun shines for us; the waters run for us; the flowers bloom for us; the grain ripens for us; and the earth teems with beauty for us all. The universe would be useless and purposeless without us. When we cease to be, there is no use for the universe or anything in it. Without us, these are virtually nonexistent. We alone give meaning, use, value, and purpose to the universe.

There is enough in the Universal One, from which all things materialize, for each of us to have enough to meet all our desires without robbing anyone else. Infinite Supply is all around us, and yet we suffer lack because most of us do not know how to claim our supply from the rich substance of the Universe.

The Law is simple, and it was laid down by the greatest political economist as well as the greatest Mental Scientist the world has in its historical records. He was not a theologian, and neither did he deal with questions of a future life, as many seem to think. He dealt with questions of life in the physical domain. His name was Jesus, and he taught his followers that the kingdom of God is within as noted in the following quote:

> *Neither shall they say, Lo here! or Lo there! For, behold, the kingdom of God is within you. (Luke 17:21 KJV).*

All things are manifestations of the One Substance, which emanates from the kingdom within. Things are, like yourself, manifestations of the One Power (God). Dollars are things. Dollars are manifestations of the One God. Most people put second things first and first things second. For instance, money, position, and influence are all secondary things; however, most people think they come first. What comes first is the power from which all secondary things emanate. First, become one with the power, and these desired things will come.

In the past, you have sown poverty seeds and are now reaping the crop. You do not enjoy this harvest. Sow, amid these results of previous sowing, plenty of seeds, and plenty will come. Supply is yours when you sow supply seeds. Sow, no matter how seemingly bleak the conditions. The seeds have God in them and cannot fail. The law of opulence is as sure as gravity. The following affirmation can help you step into a consciousness of opulence: *All is Mine! Money wants me!*

~ 8 ~

THOUGHTS THAT BRING
MONEY

Financial independence and personal liberty depend largely on the relationship between cause and effect. We can almost say that in the popular mind, the dollar confers liberty. In soul culture, a mental attitude of superiority to the dollar results in personal liberty. There is no liberty for those who feel limited by a lack of money.

Desire is the magnet. Let it have its way. Trust in your own love of truth and goodness, and never question. The fact that you desire it is enough. The fact that you desire it is evidence that it already exists for you on the soul side. Be passive toward the desire and let it manifest. This attitude is itself a success. Change your attitude toward the dollars you have. Tell them they are of no use until they are expended. As you see them lying about, say to them:

Idle dollars, you must go to work. Each one of you will

*go out and multiply. You will come back again when I
want you.*

Then let your dollars go to work for you, knowing that
when you send this thought to your money, it will return
to you manifold.

Before you spend a dollar, ask yourself, "Is it right?
Whether you spend a single dollar or a million, it makes no
difference. Therefore, when you feel it is right to spend a
dollar for any purpose, spend it as royally as if you were a
millionaire. From the inner life, this message was given to
me years ago: "Let a thought of use stand guard over your
purse and then spend freely. Amend this by affirming: "A
thought of the righteousness of the spending stands guard
over my dollars, and I send them forth with blessing."

These dollars, like every thought of good you send out,
will return to bless you. You do business with thoughts
only; dollars are just materialized thoughts. Each dollar
in your hand represents your thoughts in material form.
Send out at all times with your dollars the thoughts you
wish to return to you, for what you sow in your dollars,
you reap in dollars that either do or do not come back to
you. Put the thought of success, happiness, and health into
every dollar that passes out, and it will return so laden.

Having acquired the proper mental attitude, there is
something necessary for you to do to draw the dollar.
Your magnet of desire must have two poles. First, you
must have something that the world needs and is willing
to pay for. In this respect, you must follow the law of
supply and demand. You must honestly feel that you will

give your dollar's worth for every dollar that you desire. Secondly, you must, in all sincerity, dedicate every dollar that comes to you to noble service. You can then feel that dollars want you and that, through them, you can give what you have of value to the world. Feel that dollars wish you to use them for the accomplishment of your purpose to use them justly. With this ideal, you can conscientiously invite dollars, and they will come. They need your heart, brain, and hand so that they may benefit the world.

Dollars are manifestations of the same infinite substance as you, but, unlike you, they are not self-conscious. They have no power until you give them it. Make them feel this through your thought vibrations as you feel the importance of your work. They will then come to you to be used.

~ 9 ~

NEVER USE NEGATIVE EXPRESSIONS

Avoid negative expressions. Never use words that are not in line with your desires. Here are three expressions to avoid:

I Can't Afford It!

It is common when one desires a thing and does not feel that he can expend the cash for it to say, "I cannot afford it!" What are the dollars in your purse for? To spend? Can you afford to spend them? Is it not for that that you have them? You do not mean that you cannot afford it. This thought makes you the servant of the dollar. What you really mean is, *I do not feel that this is the best thing I can buy now. I prefer to use my money in other ways.* This is the proper attitude of mind. In it, you continue to be the master, and the dollar is subject to your decision. This may seem like a very small thing. But it is the most important thought you can apply for success. It is the thought, I tell the dollars what I want, and not, the dollars to tell what I can have! A gentleman once said to me, "I'd like to buy some of your books, but I cannot afford them! I said, "Excuse me. Do you smoke ten-cent cigars?" ($2.00 each in the 2022 economy)

"Certainly," was his reply, "at least five a day?"

"Can you afford them?"

"I can!"

"Then you will pardon me. You should have said, 'I can afford to buy some books if I decide, but I prefer to spend the money on cigars.' This is your privilege. Exercise your personal liberty, be the master of your pocketbook, and say, 'I spend money as I desire!'"

I Have Spent So Much!

This is the second expression to avoid. Have you spent or exchanged something that represented value for something of value that it stood for? You bought a suit of clothes. Twenty dollars were exchanged for clothes. In taking an account of the money, if you move twenty dollars from the cash account to assets, then your account balance is the same.

Away With It!

The third expression to avoid is *Away with it!* This is akin to the spending idea but worse. The lesson learned is worth all its costs. Nature always gives *measure for measure.* So experience for future guidance is always adequate recompense. All one gets out of life is the result of experience. Experience is the expression of life—the pressing out of life into consciousness. All of our present consciousness is the result of experience. The present is only adding, through experience, to the sum total of our consciousness. So is it true that we act with all our past and think in the present? For this reason, no one has any cause to regret, repent, or be sorry for any experience. I have learned by experience which expressions bring happiness and which bring misery. Use positive expressions about money that bring prosperity, such as those listed in the next chapter.

~ 10 ~

POSITIVE MONEY EXPRESSIONS

I recommend that the following expressions be used until the mental attitude they express becomes a belief:

- *Dollars want me.*

- *Money wants me.*

- *Bitcoins want me.*

- *All currencies want me.*

- *The indwelling power cares for my purse.*

- *I have whatever I desire.*

- *I have no question about expenditure.*

- *I purchase what I want.*

- *I can afford to use money for my happiness.*

- *I have clothes, food, books, entertainment, and whatever else I need for health, happiness, friendship, and service to others.*

- *I'm financially free.*

- *I believe that the material and spiritual person that I am will always blend for the purpose of financial success.*

- *I always have a good bank account. I actually see it. My one idea of the Law of Opulence is to use, use, use it.*

- *I use the Law of Opulence persistently until I have my full demonstration.*

- *I have strength of character, stamina, a strong backbone, and a powerful purpose in accomplishing all of my goals.*

- *I manifest money with ease for my home, business, recreation, and self-development.*

- *I have a deeper consciousness of financial freedom.*

- *I am financially free.*

Pay no attention to the old conditions. Continue your visualization and affirmations, knowing that it is the gate to the reservoir and that every irrigating ditch will fill as soon as water can come down from the reservoir to it. Financial independence comes quickly to the individual who proclaims, *Money wants me!*

ABOUT SHIRLEY A. SMOLKO

Shirley Smolko, also known as *The Venetian Medium*, is a natural Psychic Medium, which means she was born with the ability to perceive psychic information and communicate with the souls of people that have passed away. In addition to being a Psychic Medium, she is a publisher, author and lecturer.

She holds a Bachelors of Science in Nursing, a Masters in Business Administration, and another Masters degree in the Science of Accounting. She is also certified in grief counseling.

Shirley lives in the USA with her husband, Joe, and their two cats—Zoey and Cecilia. You can find out more about Shirley, her books, and what she is up to by going to: venetianmedium.com, or cavallaropub.com.

Books By Shirley Smolko (As Of This Printing):

- *My Adventures as a Psychic Nurse & Medium: Spirits Everywhere!* (Previously published as: *Adventures of a Psychic Nurse: Spirits Everywhere!*)
- *My Adventures as a Psychic Nurse & Medium: Haunted*

Hospital! (Previously published as: *More Adventures of a Psychic Nurse: Haunted Hospitals!*)

- *Just a Thought Away: Communicating With Loved Ones In Spirit*
- *Money Wants Me!*
- *Money at Your Command!*
- *Secret to the Science of Getting Rich*
- *At Your Command!*
- *Revelations of the Afterlife: A New Arrival*
- Wisdom From the Wealthy Dead: A Medium Interviews the Souls of Three American Tycoons

Be Sure to Look for Even More Books to Come!

About Henry H. Brown

Born in 1840, Henry Harrison Brown was one of the pioneers of the New Thought movement in the early part of the 20th Century. In his varied career, he taught school, worked at various newspapers, wrote books, conducted lectures, and was a Unitarian minister for seven years.

He published one of the most vigorous New Thought periodicals of his time called *Now: A Monthly Journal of Positive Affirmations,* which was devoted to Mental Science and the Art of Living. Its core affirmation was, "Man is a spirit here and now, with all the possibilities of Divinity within him and he can consciously manifest these possibilities here and now." He continued writing and lecturing until his death in 1918.

.